First Fabulous Facts

Minibeasts

Written by Jaclyn Crupi

Illustrated by Patrizia Donaera

Cartoon illustrations by Jane Porter

Consultant: Dr Kim Dennis-Bryan
Educational consultant: Geraldine Taylor

A catalogue record for this book is available from the British Library

Published by Ladybird Books Ltd
80 Strand, London, WC2R 0RL
A Penguin Company

001
© LADYBIRD BOOKS LTD MMXIII
LADYBIRD and the device of a Ladybird are trademarks of Ladybird Books Ltd

ISBN: 978-0-71819-354-6

Printed in China

Contents

What are minibeasts?

Minibeasts are creepy-crawlies. There are over a million species of minibeasts – more than any other kind of creature. Minibeasts are all different shapes and sizes. They can have lots of legs or none at all!

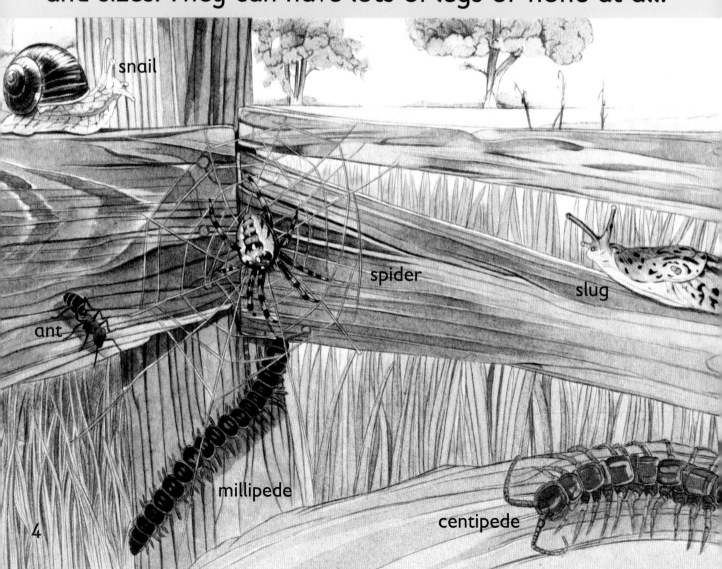

snail

spider

slug

ant

millipede

centipede

Fabulous Facts

Lots of legs

Insects always have six legs and spiders always have eight legs.

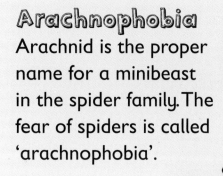

Arachnophobia

Arachnid is the proper name for a minibeast in the spider family. The fear of spiders is called 'arachnophobia'.

BOO!

Walk this way

The word 'centipede' means 'one hundred feet' but many centipedes have hundreds more legs than this.

I'll have them all!

Shoe Shop

It's not fair!

Yuck!

Snails and slugs don't have any legs. They belong to a group of animals called gastropods. Gastropod means 'stomach foot'!

Where do minibeasts live?

Minibeasts live almost anywhere. The best place to find them is where it is warm and wet – like under leaves or logs, in trees or under the ground.

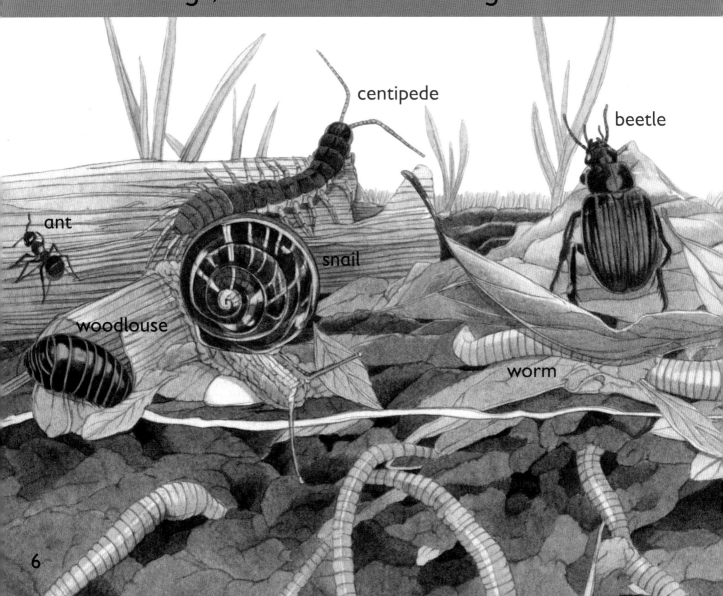

centipede

beetle

ant

snail

woodlouse

worm

Fabulous Facts

Toilet terror

Some minibeasts live near humans. The poisonous Australian redback spider often lives near toilets!

Eek!

Green unseen

The leaf insect lives among very leafy plants. By looking so much like a leaf it hides from its enemies.

Bed bugs

Minibeasts really can live anywhere. Nasty little bed bugs are never happier than when they are snuggled up in your bed!

Cosy!

Yuck!

Some minibeasts live on other creatures. For example, some fleas live on cats and dogs and headlice like to live on human heads.

Itchy!

Scratchy!

Tasty!

7

GIANT minibeasts

Some minibeasts are not really 'mini' at all! The world's largest spiders can be as big as 30 centimetres across. That is the same size as a dinner plate.

Biggest spider body

The goliath bird-eating tarantula has the largest spider body. It lives in burrows underground and feeds on insects, mice and small frogs and toads. It doesn't usually eat birds!

Longest spider legs

The giant huntsman spider has the longest spider legs. It is found in caves and usually eats insects.

Fabulous Facts

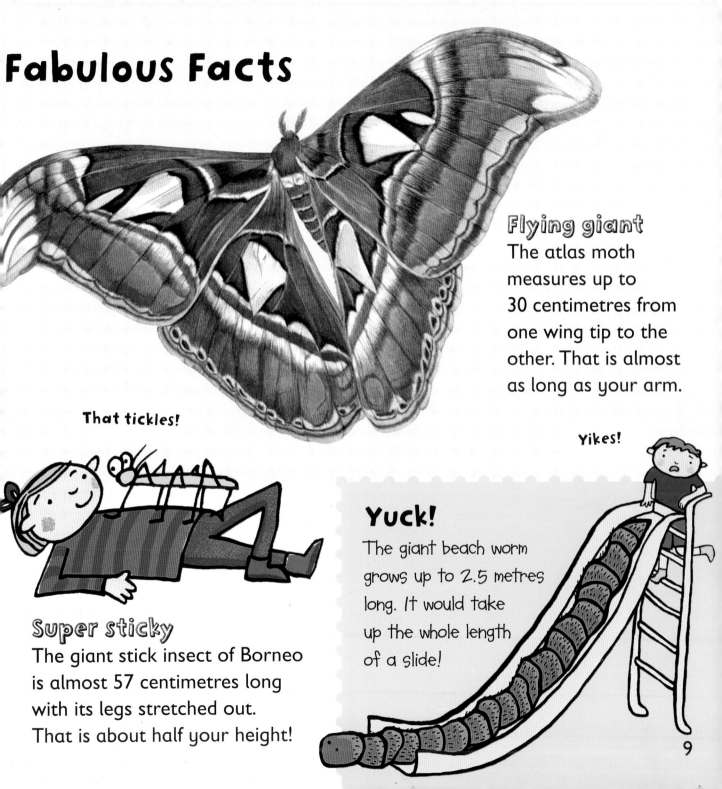

Flying giant
The atlas moth measures up to 30 centimetres from one wing tip to the other. That is almost as long as your arm.

That tickles!

Super sticky
The giant stick insect of Borneo is almost 57 centimetres long with its legs stretched out. That is about half your height!

Yikes!

Yuck!
The giant beach worm grows up to 2.5 metres long. It would take up the whole length of a slide!

TINY **minibeasts**

Most minibeasts are small, but some are tiny. Fairy flies can be as small as 0.13 millimetres long – you need a microscope to see them.

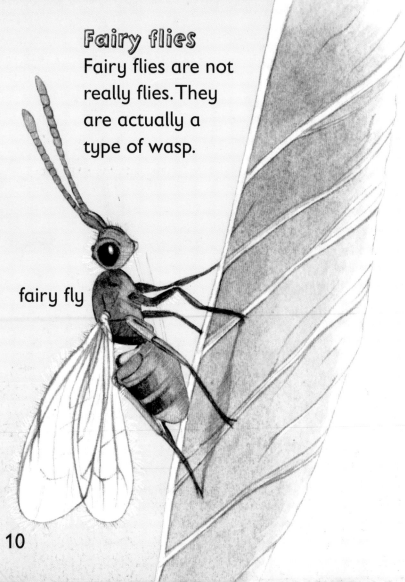

Fairy flies

Fairy flies are not really flies. They are actually a type of wasp.

fairy fly

Tiny wasp

Fairy flies are around 100 times smaller than the common wasp.

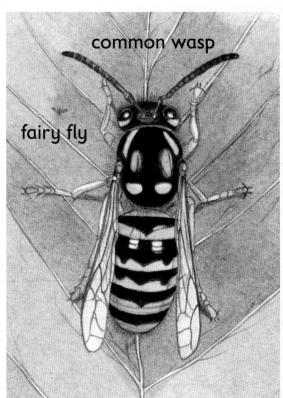

common wasp

fairy fly

Fabulous Facts

Smallest insect

Dicopomorpha echmepterygis is a type of fairy fly. It is the smallest insect with the longest name!

That's a long name!

Winged wonders

Most feather-winged beetles are less than a millimetre long.

Small is beautiful!

Smallest spider

The orbweb spider from Samoa is the size of the top of a pin.

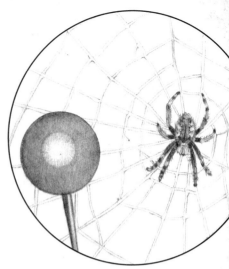

Little legs

Hoffman's dwarf centipede is only 1.3 centimetres long but it still has 82 legs.

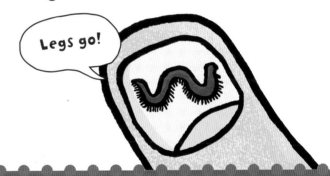

Legs go!

Yuck!

Some tiny wasps lay their eggs inside other insects' eggs. The wasp baby eats the insect baby before it has a chance to grow.

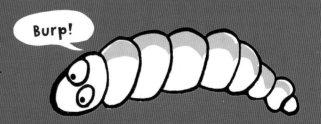

Burp!

Bug bodies

Many minibeasts have a hard outside to protect their soft bodies. Some like snails have a shell, while insects and spiders have their skeleton on the outside. An insect's body has three main parts – the head, the thorax and the abdomen.

bee

head

abdomen

thorax

Fabulous Facts

Spiral shell

As a snail's body grows, its hard shell grows with it in a beautiful spiral shape.

Eye eye!

Bees have five eyes – three small eyes on the top of their head and two large eyes at the front.

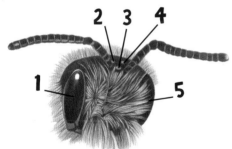

Spot the difference

How can you tell the difference between a butterfly and a moth? Butterflies' antennae have little balls on the end but moths' antennae do not.

I'm a butterfly!

I'm a moth!

That's better!

Yuck!

An insect's outside skeleton is called an exoskeleton. As it grows, an insect sheds its exoskeleton and makes a new bigger skeleton.

Bug babies

Some minibeasts are born looking a lot like they will look as an adult. Some change completely to become an adult. The monarch butterfly changes several times during its life.

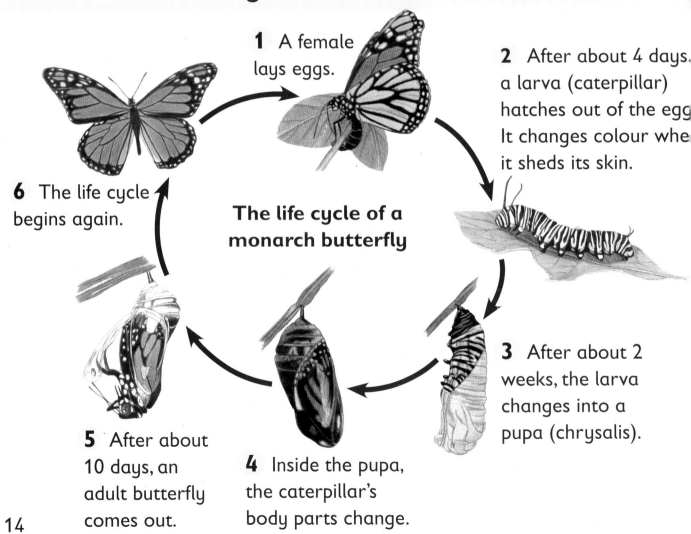

The life cycle of a monarch butterfly

1 A female lays eggs.

2 After about 4 days, a larva (caterpillar) hatches out of the egg. It changes colour when it sheds its skin.

3 After about 2 weeks, the larva changes into a pupa (chrysalis).

4 Inside the pupa, the caterpillar's body parts change.

5 After about 10 days, an adult butterfly comes out.

6 The life cycle begins again.

Fabulous Facts

Eggs everywhere

Butterflies lay their eggs on leaves, ants lay their eggs underground and some dragonflies lay them on underwater plants.

butterfly eggs

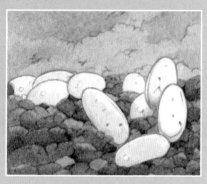
ant eggs

dragonfly eggs

Slimy babies

Slugs and snails lay up to 200 eggs at a time. They leave their eggs before they hatch.

Cool!

Yuck!

Female hissing cockroaches do not lay their eggs like other insects. The eggs hatch inside their mother's body and then the babies come out.

Water minibeasts

Some minibeasts such as beetles, dragonflies, snails and water scorpions live near water. Some lay their eggs in water. A few can even walk on water!

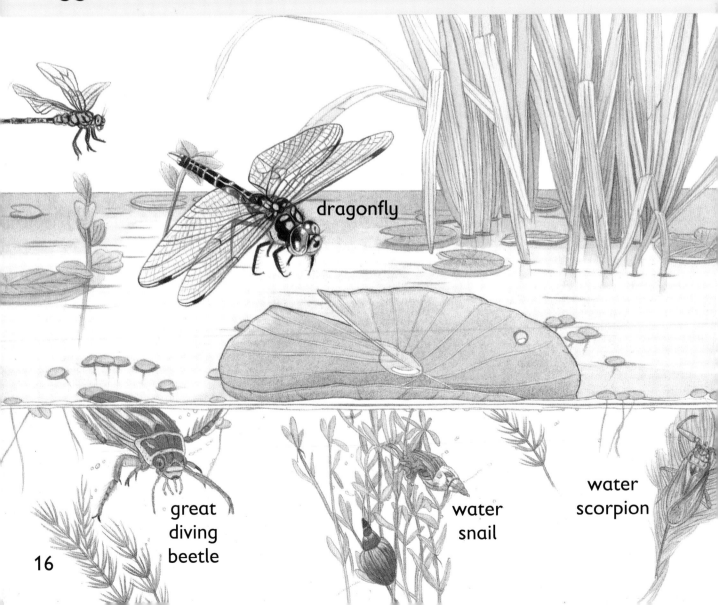

dragonfly

great diving beetle

water snail

water scorpion

Fabulous Facts

All afloat

Water striders can walk on water because they don't break its surface. The hairs on their legs trap tiny air bubbles that help them to float.

Row, row, row your boat

A water boatman swims by using its two long legs like oars on a rowing boat.

Paddle power!

Splish, splash!

Water babies

Before they become adults, some flying insects, like mosquitoes, actually live in water.

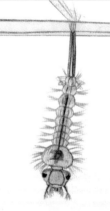

Yuck!

Water leeches are blood-suckers. They feed on blood from fish and other water creatures as well as birds and bigger animals.

I'm hungry!

I'm full!

17

Minibeasts in the air

Most flying minibeasts have four wings, but flies can only use two of their wings to fly. The other two look more like little knobs than wings. These knobs are called halteres and help the fly to steer and balance.

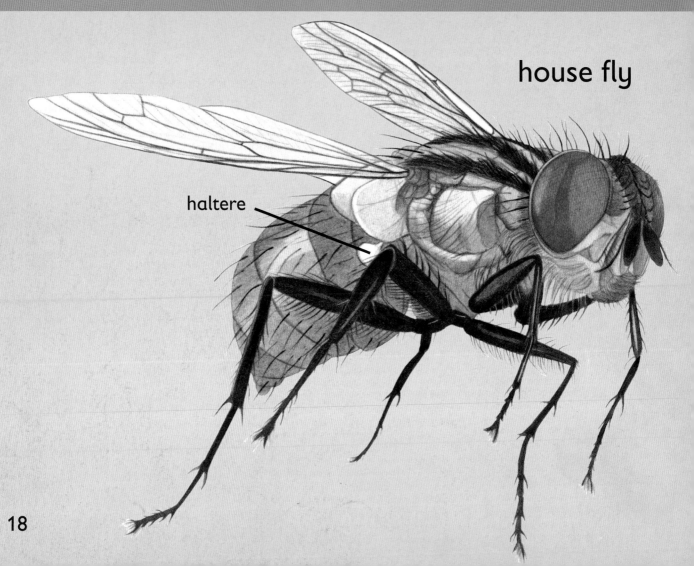

house fly

haltere

Fabulous Facts

Perfect pairs

Butterflies' front and back wings are joined and move together as one pair.

back

nt

Fantastic flappers

Dragonflies have two sets of wings which move as two pairs. They flap super fast – at about 30 times per second.

Chilling out

Insects can only fly when their wings are warm, so they fly less often in cold weather.

Brrr!

Yuck!

Butterflies taste food with their feet.

Yum!

19

Underground minibeasts

Some minibeasts live underground. Worms mix the layers of soil and let water and air through as they move around. They also leave droppings in the soil which make it very good for growing plants.

Fabulous Facts

Ant kingdom

You can make your own ant kingdom at home. A special tank will let you watch as the ants build their nest.

Wow!

Burrowing bugs

Digging bugs like ants and beetles make tunnels and burrows underground. Their tiny paths help to let water into the soil.

Bendy bodies

Worms have soft bodies with no bones, no legs and no eyes! They have bristly hairs to help them move around.

Yuck!

If a worm is accidentally cut in two, the main part of it will survive.

Oops!

Night bugs

Some minibeasts are nocturnal, which means they like to come out at night. During the day they are hidden away so you won't often see them. The firefly is a type of nocturnal beetle with wings. It gives out light from special chemicals inside its body.

moth

firefly

Fabulous Facts

Hide-and-seek

The Peruvian stick insect spends most of the day hidden under plants and only comes out at night to find food.

Midnight feast

Tarantulas hunt at night. They creep up on their prey and sink their fangs in.

Bright babies

The larvae of fireflies are called glow worms.

Yuck!

Clothes moths are most often seen at night. Although they are thought of as pests, it is the moth larva that eats holes in clothes and fabric not the adult moth.

Delicious!

23

Useful minibeasts

Some minibeasts, such as bees and ladybirds, are very useful. Bees live wherever you find flowers. As they feed, they take pollen from one flower to another. By doing this, bees pollinate the plants that make up a third of the food we eat.

beehive

honey

pollen

Fabulous Facts

The bee's knees

Pollen is a fine powder that plants need to make new plants. Pollen sticks to a bee's hairy legs and tummy as it feeds, then it rubs off on the next flower the bee visits.

Yummy honey

Bees eat a sugary liquid inside flowers called nectar. Honey bees turn nectar into honey.

Hungry helpers

Ladybirds help us by eating other minibeasts called aphids, which eat the plants we need for food.

Wow!

A honey bee will visit around 2,000 flowers a day to collect pollen and nectar.

Only 1,999 to go!

Dangerous minibeasts

Some minibeasts use deadly poison to catch their prey. Others have clever ways of protecting themselves. Some millipedes and centipedes use colour to hide from danger. Some are brightly coloured to make enemies think they taste nasty or are poisonous.

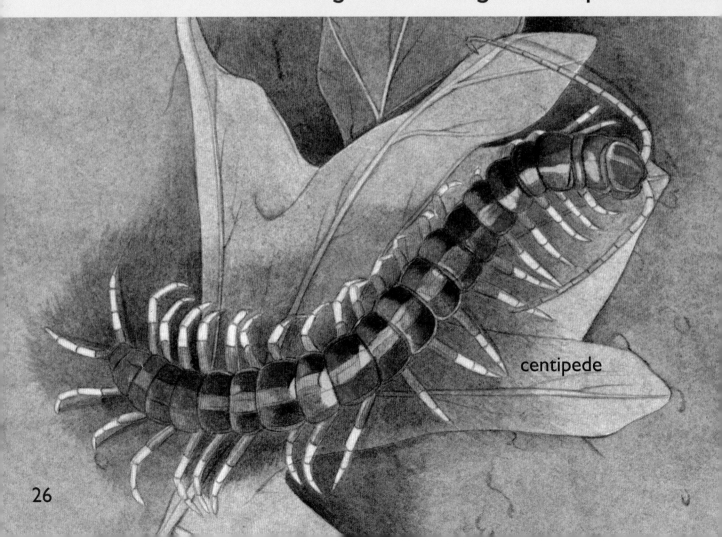

centipede

Fabulous Facts

Sting in the tail

A scorpion's tail has six parts with the stinger at the end. A scorpion uses its stinger to defend itself and sometimes to help catch and kill its prey.

stinger

Bee stings

Honey bees can only sting once. When they sting, the stinger gets stuck and breaks off and the bee dies.

stinger

Bumble bees can sting over and over again.

stinger

Yuck!

A tarantula's fangs contain poison and special chemicals that turn its prey's insides into liquid. The tarantula can then suck it up like soup!

Slurp!

Record breakers

Fastest runner

The Australian tiger beetle is the fastest running insect and can travel at 9 kilometres per hour – that's probably faster than you can run!

Heaviest insect

The larva of the goliath beetle is the heaviest insect, weighing up to 100 grams. That's about the same weight as a small apple! The adult goliath beetle is lighter. It weighs up to 60 grams.

Loudest insect

The African cicada is probably the loudest insect. They use songs to communicate and find a mate. They might also use sound to defend themselves.

Largest eggs

The eggs of carpenter bees are among the largest insect eggs. They are 16.5 millimetres long and 3 millimetres wide.

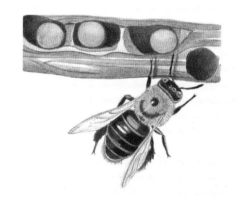

Smallest eggs

The smallest insect eggs are the tiny eggs of Tachinidae, which are only up to 0.2 millimetres long.

eggs

Funny bugs!

What is the biggest ant in the world?

An eleph-ant!

How do you start an insect race?

One, two, flea... Go!

How do headlice email one another?

Over the internit!

Where do bees go to catch a bus?

The buzz stop!

How did the sick insect get to hospital?

In an ant-bulance!

What's green and wriggly and never shuts up?

A chatterpillar!

Glossary

antenna   A feeler which an insect uses to feel, smell, taste and hear. More than one antenna are called **antennae**.

burrow   A hole or tunnel in the ground where minibeasts live.

chrysalis   A shell where an insect changes from a baby to an adult.

egg   A hard shell with a new baby creature inside.

fangs   The mouth parts of a spider which it uses to hold its prey and inject poison into it.

hatch   To break out of an egg.

larva   A baby insect. More than one larva are called **larvae**.

life cycle   The stages of a creature's life.

pollination   When pollen is taken from one flower to another. Pollination allows plants to make seeds which will turn into new plants.

prey   Creatures that are hunted by other creatures for food.

pupa   Another word for chrysalis.

skeleton   All the bones in a body.

soil   The top covering of the ground.

species   A group of animals or plants that are the same.

Index